*for Niall, Cian
and Ronan*

ACKNOWLEDGEMENTS

Acknowledgements are due to the following publications in which a number of these poems first appeared:

Poetry Ireland Review, *Poetry Australia*, *The Steeple*, *Northlight* (Scotland), *The Frontier Post* (Twickenham), *Poesis* (Romania), *The Anglo Celt*, *Longford Leader*, *The Connacht Tribune*, *Leitrim Observer*, *The Spark*, *Force Ten*, *Windows Broadsheet* and *Windows Selection*.

Also the producers of The Poet's Chair and The Arts Programme, (RTE radio).

My thanks to the Tyrone Guthrie Centre, Annaghmakerrig where the collection began.

A special thanks to John Montague, Evelyn Conlon and Heather Brett for their interest and advice.

CONTENTS

I – GIRL ON A TRAPEZE

II – AUTUMN CONCERTO

I

GIRL ON A TRAPEZE

We were staring up
At her crescent flight
Our heads rolling over and back,
Lost in her composure,
Her shapely body shining
Throwing shadows on the canvas
Above the lights.

For years I saw her swing
Across silence on Sundays
Or from fluorescent lights
In the study-hall, switch swings
In flight, defiantly smiling,
Moonwitching my head for heights
Over and back,

            From memory to impulse.

CURLS

Before the gold wore off
You cut my first curls,
Folding them carefully in paper,
You posted them in a cleft

In the apple tree.
Your letter moving further inside,
Past applewood rings
To the heart of the heartwood.

Little lunulae letter
I can always read you
Through the lichen door.

OUTSIDE PEIG SAYERS' HOUSE

In Dunquin, I stood in the yard
Facing the sheep grazing mountains
The mist coming down.

Your house was at my back, Peig,
Old Potato Face, as we called you
At school, reluctant to read
Your chapters of hardship.

Thinking back you were always
A natural for work and prayer
And I wondered if, even once,
You let these mountains near you,
The fiery fuchsias overtake you,
Their long red tongues hanging out
And did you run along snow quarts,
Sure-footed in your bare feet,
Roll in self-heal, wild thyme, bright eye,
Before hardship overtook you.

You were never one for choices, Peig,
A Blasket marriage wedded you
To the village above White Strand,
To the undertow of the seals' tune,
The fear of Fatal Cliff,
Fishing and potato digging
And more chapters of hardship surfacing.

And when the island closed down,
You returned to this stream
Running across the yard,
A currach below a potato garden
Tarry side up.

As the German tour pulled off
I went inside.
It was a stage set, saccharine sweet.
They had flaked off the old paint,
Cramped the kitchen with props.

No. 30, Crannard Road

Hedges. Islands of lawns
On concrete pavement.
The car pulls up at No. 30.
It's time to unload
The cases, explore the rooms
Finger the staircase.

Summer here is mornings
When dressing is put off
Till after breakfast and day trips
Are planned, glimpsing out
At shifting clouds
From the kitchen window.

Out past limestone walls
We drive to quiet beaches
With picnic baskets full
And spread the rug and eat
And listen and walk
The shoreline, feel the sand dislodge

Beneath our feet. Rainfall.
The hullabaloo of the children
Running upstairs. The sitting-room,
A quiet retreat where bride and groom
And invited guests with mouth smiles
For the camera look down from the piano

At your house arrest. Nightfall.
Weariness turns into dreams.
Sea-shells, seagulls curl
On a cloud's edge, someone coughs,
The baby swallows milk
And slips into another dream.

Leaf-fall. Rowan-berry ripeness
On the pavement. Swallows cluster
On the wires. The cases are packed
In the car. An ice-lolly paper
Darts down the road.
The slowness of summer is over.

EPIPHANY

From this node of ash
A windfall, lying on the road,
I see your figure emerge,
Crowned in black buds
Sweatless and sapless
Severed at the omphalos,
Your right arm longer than the left,
Pulled to one side from Rome.
And I lay you to rest
On a gossamer trampoline,
Where old thistle heads stand round
Losing their hair in a September wind
Hoping some day you'll bounce back to me,
In the words of a prayer or a poem.

ALONE IN THE FIELDS

When I was small
I met God The Father
In the tenterfields
And I asked Him
About the shape of thorns
On the wooden frame,
The eel in the mill-river.

He filled his pipe with tobacco,
Puffed smoke into his woolly beard
And told me:
Ropes were first made
By men walking backwards.

SUNDAY PEOPLE

After worship and Sunday dinner
Husbands creak along the road
In bronze boots, iron caps. Wives
With white enamel smiles
Push prams past cottages
Where old people cuddle gates
Stretch arms across the bars for handshakes.

                         Family meets family
Unrefined ferrite looks from the men
Who pull at their caps,
Check their shirt studs. Mothers
Baby-talk to each other's baby,
Discuss food, medicines. Brassy children
File away at their parents' patience.

Running ahead
I leave their adult conversations
About iron crowns and parish glory
And see their gossip chains
Dissolve:
        Link by link
Hear the metal of their shadows

As they round the turn
And head for home,
Past umbrian fields of soldered leaves
On sentinel trees, pig-iron hills on either side
Holding my Sunday people
In the grip of custom
And grinding them to a halt . . .

Now, almost silent
Except in my dreams, I hear the gong
Of their heartbeats, on the tight wire of sleep.

THE RUSSIANS ARE COMING

The Russians are coming tomorrow
Godless Russians coming on Saturday
To stir up trouble
When the school is closed,
I wish it was tomorrow.

They'll rope all the moneymakers
And everything from bibles, green almanacs, brylcream . . .
Will be listed down in red books,
Teetotallers forced to drink Vodka,
Bachelors and spinsters compelled to nod at each other.

There'll be three dark days
Before they come, Sr. Concepta
The solemn nun said:
And when the Russians arrive
We'll no longer be human.

Mrs. Blaney will pour them tea
And feed them buns with damson jam,
Rosie will straighten her nylon seams,
Cissie Brady will read from the horoscope
And prepare herself for surprises.

And all the men who worked,
And all the men who never worked,
Will go goose-stepping into the morning,
Their shiny reaping hooks
Edging above their shoulders along the sky.

And by evening when they return,
The space age will have begun,
With spirals of sputniks
Going to the moon,
From the hill overlooking the town.

The Russians are coming tomorrow,
Godless Russians coming on Saturday,
There'll be so much happening,
So many new things to do . . .
They better come tomorrow.

WORDFARMING

I was driven out tonight
Mooned by some strange love
To listen for the roots of words
And the speech of little stones
Under the stars.

MILKING

When you sat
legs supporting a bucket
I listened to the white liquid lines

And when they crossed
to make an x,
you told me
it was a white kiss,

Fresh and frothy,
electrifying the metal
with a current that passed
through me and earthed.

PEGGED ON THORNS

Were old coats, red flannel,
Plaid shawls. Signs from departed travellers
To those arriving, that such a byroad
Made good camping ground.

And when a cow gave birth
To a heifer-calf
My father threw the afterbirth
To thorny heights
To cast a spell
Runecraft a bull-calf down
The next time round.

Canopies on the hedges
Splayed above me. The lid
On my childhood lifted
When they faded and withered.

II

Autumn Concerto

Autumn Concerto

i

Crowds of goblin leaves
Have taken the gold ring
Down from the trees
In a flurry of leaf melody,
Split its light:
          And dance
Along the road in its colours:
To the shriek of a chain-saw
Starting up, the hammer strokes
Of a farmer fencing
Beating out – his line – of land,
A robin's phrase
Spells out his territory
In a cadenza of scolding scale,
Somewhere deep in the wood
A chugging tractor underpins the melody.

ii

Three muted swans on the lake,
Lost in the mournful after-sounds
Of a solo oboe in the reeds,
Ducks' aqua music,
The airy vowels
Of children playing
At the water's edge.

iii

In the final movement,
Peeping stars make bony notes
On the xylophone of sitka-spruce
In the forest.
A sparrow-hawk
Timing his entry with precision
Swoops down on the shadowy side
And dances a forlana
With a most reluctant field-mouse.

White Nocturne

The night
Will not lie down.

I hear
A little old lady
Weeping in fields
Of unknown snow.

I see her
Run to the edge
Fade into a space of silence.

CANDLE

Milkrush at evening
Show me your shadow
On the tallowy field.

Leafspear of light
Trembling in the dark
Cradle my fear.

Waterlily at midnight
Pillow my dreams
In your oily well.

Snakeroot of smoke
At daybreak
Incense the morning.

NIGHT

When ash limbs beat
On slate and glass
In the house
Of the bed and grave,
The whores and virgins
In flames of flesh
Swim past the Gates of Glory,

Lipping and kissing
On the river bed,
Deep in sodalite sand,
Their breasts hanging, hurricane-lamps
In the stormy currents of sleep.

November Lake

All that talk
About bobbing about in a boat,
Men fishing men
And water in stone jars, wet
Your bone dry roots,
Draped you in black leaf
And vows flowered inside you.

    Alone in that thistle choking parish
    They gave you,
              Your fugal flights
    Of black and white
              Your left hand
    Shouting down your right,
                 Not even
    The scent of a woman at the well.

The stones could have been loaves
When you drove there
And the wind a bubble chain of breath
Novembering on the waves,
As you walked along
The out of line steps
Into a winter lake
And there under the great weight of water
You found all the tears
For your feet.

What stirrings on the lake bed
When divers brought you in
Bearing up their netful
Through the reeds.

COLDLY THE FIRST FLAKES

Coldly the first flakes
Swan about before they nest,
Stippling the wall-moss and lawn.

And a wind warms up behind the trees
To threshing force, corn-snow everywhere,
War whooping cries and hedges
Wild with winter music.

Nightfall and still the battle rages,
Moon-seeds flying past,
Chasing, colliding, tumbling into furrows
And the wind calls off the fray
When white has overtaken night.

Next morning, a mute robin who spent summer
Field-preaching in the garden,
Comes into an out-house
Spellbound by the sleeping snow.

ROBIN

Blood-breasted gospel preacher
Rigid in the bush,
When the wind unveils
your whitish underparts, you fly
To another thorny spot
Intone the same chant
In the rain, afraid to discover
Your own sex.

Little moral pretender,
You'd quarrel with your brother
Over a haw or a worm
Or the right of way to drinking water
And when the permafrost comes,
you'll arrive at my sill
With that pious look of yours
Expecting charity.

BUD CLUSTERS

At the end of twigs
Were wild animals' feet
In a leafless winter world
That turned the animal kingdom

On its back:
Each bough, a leg
Pawing the dark, the stars
Their footprints in the night.

SNOWFIRE

Billions of white stamens went slinking
Past the window
Closing up the fields
The cold winter roads.

When I opened the window
The white desert entered
And burnt me inside.

THE SNOWWOMAN

She stood on the square
A feral ice figure
With strawen hair, snowwhite breasts
Hay-thatch on her crotch.

Nobody ignored her:
They all thought it shameful
To have her standing in the pelt
In broad day light.
The priest informed them
There wasn't any mention of it
In Canon Law, since Canon Law
Was codified in the hot countries
Where there're no snowfalls.
Perhaps it's a civil matter, he said.
The Urban Council felt
It was part of our culture
And winter celebrations
To erect a snowman
But a snowwoman
In this shape and size
Was a contumacious act.
While the powers that be
Were deciding who'd decide
What best to do
A young bravado
Returning from a disco
Swore he'd defile her
While his friends watched.

Unfamiliar with the cold facts
And rhythms of a snowwoman
He failed to ruffle her composure,
Penetrate her white panoply.
Looking into her charcoal eyes
He could feel himself begin to melt
And he shied away from the encounter.

Next morning tongues were flails
Threshing the young brat's behaviour
And the whole town was alive with rumours.
One question led to another
But condemnation wavered
When someone asked
Who put her there to taunt him?
Suspects were called to mind
But before they could
Pin the blame on anyone
The sun came out
And took her down to the river.

Later she rejoined the sun
In his humid kingdom
Out of reach of everyone.
But her presence is felt,
Her hair hangs from a lamp post
Her eyes look up from the square
And as she drifts past in the clouds
The town's children look up and say
There goes the blind snowwoman
Who'll return to our square.

CHRISTMAS IN THE WEST

The night smells of whiskey,
Clouds of cigarette smoke rise
Above the beads of Christmas lights
On aslant streets. Mothertown, bride
To the wind and rain
Is mad with people home for Christmas.

Pint glasses chime in *The Green Piano*,
Phatic conversations, every word
A fairy light in the dark lounge,
Body curves touch, hands hoop familiar waists,
Drink comes with ice.
High-stoolers, elbows on the counter,
Vacate their metal thrones to trot to the Men's.

It's two a.m.
Everyone ignores the coloured TV,
Laughing doors open into alleyways,
Taxi doors slam in the holly berry dawn
Of Christmas morn.

Candles flicker on linen,
Bare hands, fingers twisted in fire,
Three camels eat silage outside,
Weather-prophets stand on their heads
Looking for a star in the East.

It's a bungee jump, a quick splash
For Christmas and they're gone,
Ferrying their dreams
As far as they care to go.
January takes a bite out of the town,
It's all peaceful again,
Silent nights . . . Holy nights . . .

THE SAME CHILD

Here we are again
In our separate places,
You in the finery of your stained glass
And me with my Graeco-Roman look

On Christmas night. Inside
We both house the same child
Destined for the same cross
And the one star lights us up,

While we stand our ground
Gazing at each other,
On opposite sides of the road
In an Ulster town, in the South.

III

THE UNDERCURRENT

THE UNDERCURRENT

Words swim past
Out near the end
Where unhealed quarrels
Clipped to stone
Waver in the undercurrent of memory.

Pain is at work here:
Trapped between God and man
My words snipe at both
And I pare my lines down to the bone,

Watch the shavings surface,
Ponder the endless possibilities
Before I swim out from the Irish Sea
To rest on a lone white rock
Somewhere between whale music
And the aching eel-grass in the undercurrent.

In Dublin's Fair City

In the name of Science, Humanism and Reason
                                    she says:

Come to my centre.
Come in from the cold circumference
Of the colloquial and coin
City words, current words for my capital.

In the name of Science, Humanism and Reason
                                    she says:

Avoid unholy communion
With your past, your small townishness
Your provincial accent, your running off
To funerals of the small farmers.

In the name of Science, Humanism and Reason
                                    she says:

Take this Hamburger and eat it,
For this is the universal food.
Take this Pepsi and drink it,
For this is the ichor of the future.

In the name of Science, Humanism and Reason
                                    she says:

Have a passion for my granite,
The gulls shrieking on my water,
The delirium of my sleeplessness
As I prostrate before you tonight.

In the name of Science, Humanism and Reason.

THE BISHOP'S BELL AT INCH

I hear the bishop's bell
In the cuckoo oats,
The metal run in the rocks
Ringing, from the white meadow
Down to the red wheat by the sea.

I hear the ding-dong
Of a love prayer
That turned to play.
The tam-tam of a crozier
On a feather-star,
The sand-eel striking.

I hear bells echoing everywhere,
Tongue tips clanging,
The bell-founder
Can't be found,
The bell rope
Twisted in cuckoo oats
Down to the red wheat by the sea.

A Plea for a Part in the Divine Comedy

Father! Father! Can I round up the dues
In small brown envelopes and supervise
The bread-basket collections at Mass.

Father! Father! Let me sing in the choir
My confessions of guilt and remorse
Me-a-cowboy, Me-a-cowboy, Me-a-Mexican-cowboy.

Father! Father! Give me respectability
Put my name on the Sunday Bulletin
On the Lenten, Pentecostal and all other Holy Bulletins.

Father! Father! Fax me into Rome
Let me have a first copy
Of the New Universal Catechism.

Father! Father! Mitre and crozier me
Let me lep on a lorry
For the St. Patrick's Day pageant.

Father! Father! Make me renounce
Druids and learning and poets
And be faithful to the clipped words of the community.

Father! Father! Blackmail me into subjection
Let me be part of your divine comedy
Sublimate me.

WHEN THE PIGS WERE HOLY COWS IN BLACK JAMES'S TOWN

This is the town
Where the pork-festival
Almost happened
And this little piggy
Nearly jumped on the bandwagon
And that little piggy
Nearly stayed at home
And all the pig-farmers
Who sometimes drive fish
From the streams, the rivers and lakes
And are known to make money their God,
Could scarcely, Weep! Weep! Weep!
All the way home.

FATE OF A KEPT MAN

Patrick's father was everything
Hand-outs supreme
And Patrick and his wife Bridie lived happily
And never had to work and never wanted.

One day of everyday
Patrick lay stretched in the grass
Perfectly happy and perfectly bored.
Bridie approached him
Cajoling him with kisses
To do something different.

Patrick filled with the boredom
Of a kept man agreed
And they did something.

Patrick's father was raging
Threw the pair of them out
As the first thunder storm came in from the Atlantic.

Wet and soggy
Up to their navels in bog-water
They covered their peat stained bodies in heather
And hardened into work
Unravelling the undergrowth
And foraging for words.

Patrick's father was present in his absence
Revealed himself while they slept,
Mental-flashing in his room outside,
Making them mad with guilt,
Driving them to islands and mountain streams
To launder their souls in prayer.

Patrick and his wife Bridie
Have lived for thousands of years,
They have forgotten the boredom of keepdom
And are saving up grace
To return to Patrick's father's place.

LITHOMANIA

We played soldiers
Squadrons of us
Hauling one another out of the sea
Roaring like thunder
Rolling over and back.

We grew up together,
Pressing, touching, rubbing
Each other in a courtship
That gave smoothness
To our wet nakedness.

You lay on the beach
A perfect limestone figure
Big and small in the right places
And I fell
Stone madly in love with you.

We got ourselves a wall
Away from the sea. Got wedged
Into a quiet drumlin neighbourhood
Up to our eyes in erosion
All proper limestones in proper limestone places.

Now that we're old stones
With hair-cracks on our faces
We can afford to retire
To a drystone wall in the West
And let the yowling wind come between us.

LEVELS

Once in a while
I go down slowly
To breathe out of oxygen's reach
Deep in rootfree soil
Away from the nearness of window changes
In the little shops and houses
Hardly aware of the foot-patrol above.

I owe this poem to a raindrop
That crushed its way
Along stone and clay
Through layers of amber and brown
And through its lens:
I can see the formation of wild geese

Carry time solemnly
Above the little shops and houses
                              Across the sky.

In the Undercover

A will-o'-the-wisp dances
Along a constellation of pebbles
To the piccolo of raindrops.
And I am of one mind
In three tenses,
Past, Present and Future,
Looking out from the undercover,
Waiting for the rain to clear.

A Change of Mood

Silken threads of rain
Shock the river
Into glassy stitches of laughter.

And when the shower eases,
The silver fibres lull
Into vowel drops
And sad concentric circles
Sing to me.

School Children

I see them
Through an open cube
Of winter light
That sits on a bleak lawn
Between two windows.

Obscured by condensation,
Their vague shapes move
As if on a Monet canvas,
Bluish strokes elbowing their way,
School ties are ripples, piled-up books
In their arms, driftwood,
In some half crazy river
Flowing past into Bedlam.

And when the electric bell
Penetrates the morning,
They'll flood these empty rows
With fury and purpose.

What words can I give them
To put on their pages?

MOUNT JOSEPH

This is a home
With TV rooms and lounges
And wall paint that soothes.

A falling asleep place between meals
Where doctors and nurses keep death
At bay and dying comes slowly

To eyes that look out at me
From wheel-chairs, beds and I bow
To a vase of roses to lose their stare.

Frail tired people, ready to sleep
Before the moon comes out,
With skin like bark about their bones.

On the corridor, an old man
Taps his way, echoing the here-and-now
Of the down-to-earth call:

Open the window
And let the soul out.

STONE CIRCLE

We followed the bog path
To the great stone circle,
A keepsake of these hills.

Here the wind quarrels
With anything standing
Bush and stone, all subjects
To its wailing power.

On impulse:
We joined hands,
Spun each other around,
Excited to a frenzy
We lay down
And felt the great stonewheel
Move around us.

Rotating boulders
Went slooping past
Like sharks about their prey,
Their great limestone tails
Rounding the squareness of our lives.

LARGE WHITE

I am a wild flying flower
Bolder and brighter now
I delight in my strange white.

In my other lives
I was egged on,
Knowing somehow
I was meant for flight.

I became a nettle worm
In a boarding school,
Ate prescribed passages
Till I was slimy green in the face
And on the point of bursting
I moulted.

I clung to lady's bedstraw
With the local pupae,
Biding my time
In a leafy hillside village
That nicknamed me *cabbage white*.

I have all the fun
In the sunlight.
I love my flights,
The tumbling froth of wings,
Above the village spire,
A honeymoon on an ice plant fire.

I am the white ghost of night,
Perched on the inside of a leaf
I write white poems
With the milky ink of the stars.